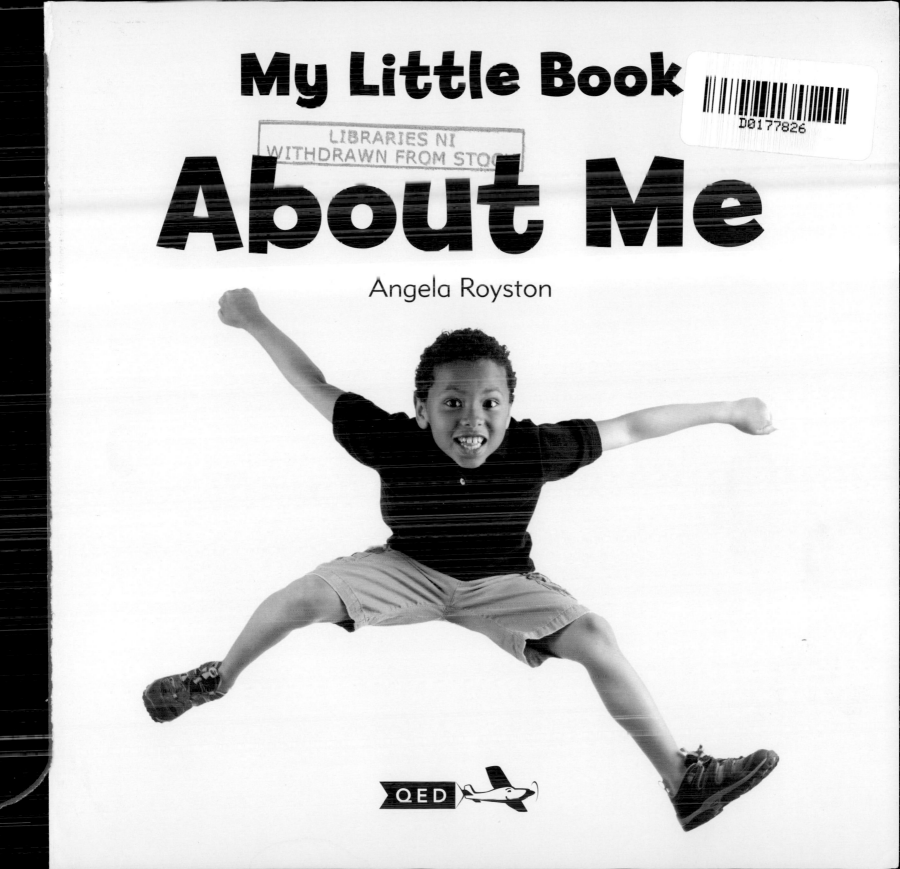

My Little Book

About Me

Angela Royston

QED

Quarto is the authority on a wide range of topics.

Quarto educates, entertains and enriches the lives of our readers—enthusiasts and lovers of hands-on living.

www.quartoknows.com

Publisher: Maxime Boucknooghe
Editorial Director: Victoria Garrard
Art Director: Miranda Snow
Project Editor: Sophie Hallam
Design and editorial: Tall Tree Ltd

First published in the UK in 2016 by
QED Publishing
Part of the Quarto Group
The Old Brewery, 6 Blundell Street, London N7 9BH

www.quartoknows.com/brand/979/QED-Publishing/

A catalogue record for this book is available from the British Library

ISBN 978 1 78493 470 5

Printed in China

Words in **bold** are explained in the glossary on page 60.

Contents

Inside and out

My body is made up of many different parts. They include my arms, legs, head, fingers and toes.

« I run by moving my legs, feet and arms.

⌃ I use my hands, eyes and ears to play the guitar.

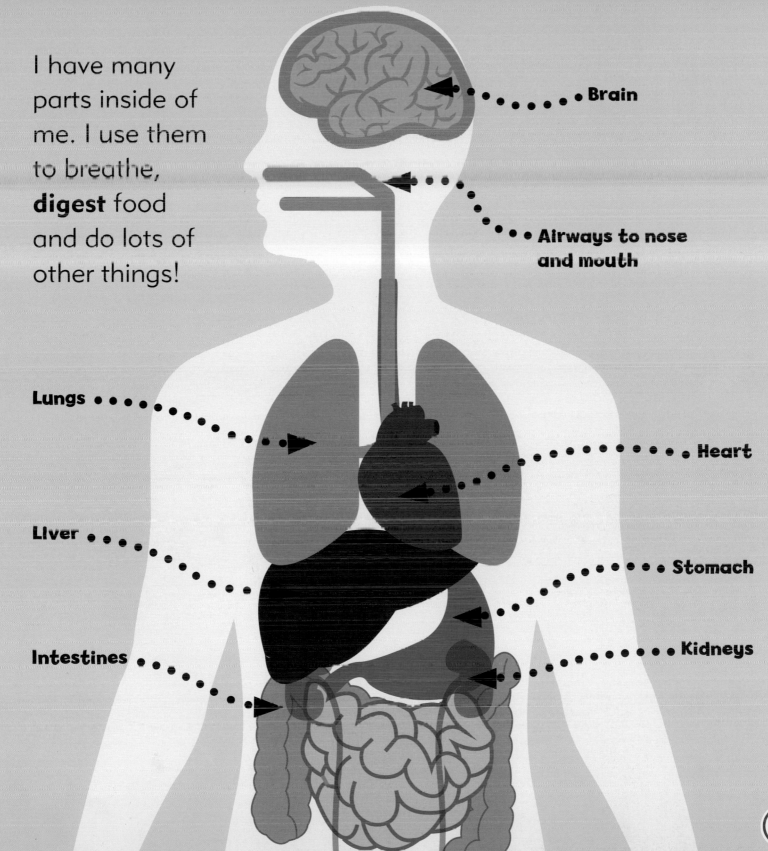

I have many parts inside of me. I use them to breathe, **digest** food and do lots of other things!

Brain

Airways to nose and mouth

Lungs

Heart

Liver

Stomach

Intestines

Kidneys

The world and me

My face connects me to the world. I see with my eyes, and I use my teeth, tongue and lips to form words.

⌄ I taste food in my mouth and smell it with my nose.

« I talk to my cat and listen to her purr.

I need air, food and water to stay alive. My nose and mouth take in air, and my mouth takes in food and drink.

« My eyes, nose and ears tell me what is going on around me.

• • Eye

• • Ear

• Nose

• • Mouth

Inside my head

My **brain** is my body's control centre.
My **senses** send information to
my brain along **nerves**.

>> **Nerves from every part of my body go up my spinal column to my brain.**

Spinal column

Nerve

My brain is like a super-computer that makes sense of the outside world, and controls what happens inside me.

∨ My brain takes up just 2 per cent of my body's weight, but it uses 20 per cent of my body's energy!

>> My brain is incredibly complex. It contains 100 billion tiny nerve cells.

Seeing

I see when light enters my eye through the black hole in the centre. This hole is called the **pupil**. The **iris** controls the amount of light entering the eye.

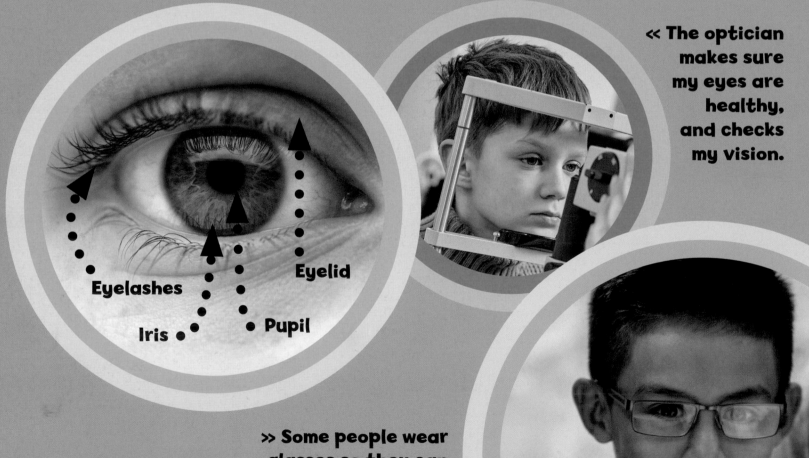

Eyelashes

Eyelid

Iris

Pupil

<< The optician makes sure my eyes are healthy, and checks my vision.

>> Some people wear glasses so they can see more clearly.

The light forms a moving picture inside
my eye. The picture is upside-down,
but my brain sees it the right way up!

**Upside-down
image of object**

Object

Lens

**Nerve to
brain**

^ The lens **bends the light to make a
clear picture on the back of my eye.
A nerve carries the picture to my brain.**

Hearing

When something makes a noise, **sound waves** spread out all around it. I hear when sound waves reach my ears.

Sound waves

Outer ear

Ear channel

« A drum vibrates when it is hit. This means that it shakes very fast and produces sound waves.

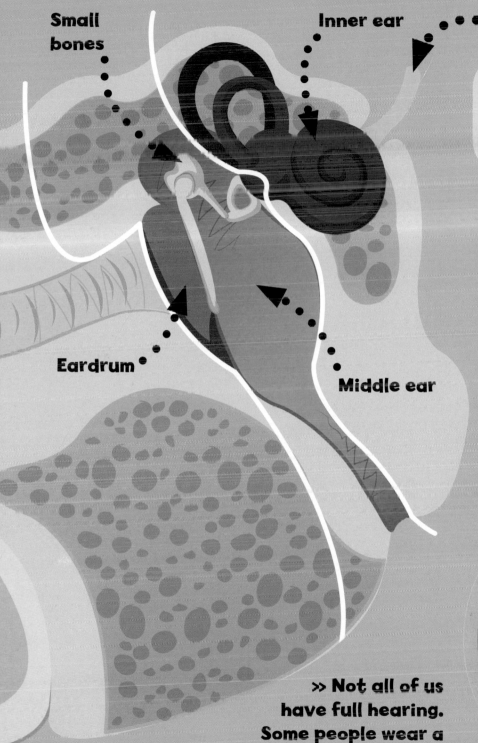

Small bones

Inner ear

Nerve to brain

Eardrum

Middle ear

<< Most of my ear is protected inside my skull.

Sound waves pass down the ear channel to the **eardrum**. They keep going until they reach the nerve in my inner ear, which sends a message to my brain.

>> Not all of us have full hearing. Some people wear a hearing aid to help them hear.

13

Taste and smell

I taste when **chemicals** in my food reach my tongue. My tongue has **taste buds** that pass messages to my brain.

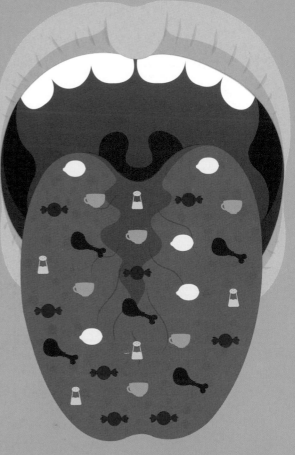

⌄ My tongue has thousands of taste buds. They detect five basic tastes: sweet, sour, bitter, salty and savoury.

« Taste and smell work together to help me enjoy my favourite treats.

I smell when chemicals in the air reach my nose. Nerves deep inside my nose tell my brain about the smell.

Smell nerves

Brain

˄ My nose can identify more than 10,000 different scents.

Air goes through my nose

Chemicals in the air

Touch

Every part of my skin contains nerves. These give me a sense of touch that keeps me aware of my surroundings.

>> Nerves near the skin's surface detect a light touch. Deeper nerves tell me when I've hurt myself.

<< My fingertips have so many nerves that I can feel every bump and ridge on a surface.

⌄By dipping my toe in the pool, I can tell how cold the water is. I can sense even small changes in temperature.

When I hurt myself, nerves send a pain message to my brain. Pain is important as it helps me to avoid dangerous things.

Skin

Skin covers my body. It protects my insides from the world outside. Skin stops dirt and germs getting inside of me.

Hairs grow through skin

« Sun cream helps to stop skin from being burned by the sun.

Layer of fat

Epidermis

Dermis

My skin is **waterproof**. It is covered with tiny, hard flakes and is slightly oily. The oil keeps the water out. Skin has a tough outer layer called the epidermis, and an inner layer called the dermis. Under the skin is a layer of fat.

Hair and nails

More than 100,000 hairs grow on my head! Every day, about 100 hairs fall out and are replaced by new hairs.

« Hair keeps my head warm when it is cold and helps to cushion my skull.

» Hair can be curly or straight. Some people have dark hair, others have fair or red hair.

^ Healthy fingernails are smooth and made from layers of a protein called keratin.

Hard, flat nails protect the tips of my fingers and toes. I cut my fingernails with clippers to stop them growing too long.

Too hot or too cold?

When I am hot, I **sweat**. Drops of salty liquid ooze from tiny holes in my skin. As the sweat dries, it cools my skin.

>> Playing sport makes me hot and thirsty. A drink of water helps to cool me down.

<< When I am ill my temperature may rise, making me sweat.

When I'm cold, **muscles** in my body shake, making me shiver. The energy of shivering creates heat that helps keep me warm.

« Thick clothes help to keep me warm.

^ Goosebumps form when tiny muscles pull my hairs upright. These warm me, like a thin sleeve.

Bones

Bones are the hard parts inside my body. Everybody has the same bones. They make us human-shaped!

Skull

Spine

Pelvis

>> My skeleton has 206 bones! About half of them are in my hands and feet.

⌄ My ribs form a protective cage.

Some bones protect important parts of the body. For example, my ribs protect my heart and **lungs**. The skull is a bony helmet that protects my brain.

⌄ The jaw bone forms my chin and holds my bottom teeth.

Rib cage

Skull

Jaw

Joints

A **joint** is a place where two or more bones meet. Bones cannot bend, but joints allow them to move in different ways.

˅ I use the joints in my legs, feet, arms and back when I run.

« I bend my legs at my hips, knees and ankles when I crouch down.

My hips and shoulders are ball and socket joints. They let me move my legs and arms in a circle. My knees and fingers have hinge joints so I can only bend and straighten them.

˄ I use joints in my shoulders, elbows and wrists when I hit a ball.

My hip has a ball and socket joint.

My knee has a hinge joint.

My ankle has a gliding joint so bones can move from side to side.

Muscles

Without muscles, I would not be able to move. My bones move because they are pulled by my muscles.

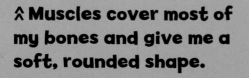

⌃ **Muscles cover most of my bones and give me a soft, rounded shape.**

>> Muscles in my face move my mouth and cheeks. My tongue is a muscle too!

Muscles are attached to bones by tendons. I sit on my biggest muscles – my buttocks. They cushion my bottom!

>> Muscles in my upper arm move my lower arm at the elbow.

This muscle bends my arm.

Tendon

Elbow joint

This muscle straightens my arm.

Amazing hands

My hands are amazing!
I use my thumb and fingers
to draw, cut with scissors and
make small, careful movements.

« I use my thumb
and fingers to write.

« My hand has 27 bones. The muscles that move these bones are all in my lower arm.

My fingers can only bend and straighten, but my thumb can make circular movements. Only humans, apes and some monkeys can do this.

⌃ When I practise the piano, my fingers work together to play the keys.

Breathing

When I breathe in, I take in air through my nose or mouth. The air contains a gas called **oxygen**, which I need to stay alive. Oxygen enters my body through my lungs.

⌃ I can see my breath in the air on cold days. My breath contains water, which forms small droplets when it's cold.

≪ When I sneeze, I blast air out through my nose. Sneezing pushes out dust and germs.

» When I swim, I need to lift my head out of the water to breathe in air.

Nose

Mouth

Windpipe

Lungs

Narrow airways

Air travels from my nose or mouth into a large tube called the windpipe. The windpipe looks like a vacuum hose. It splits into two tubes, one to each lung. The tubes then divide into narrow airways that carry air into the lungs.

The lungs

Lungs take up most of the space inside my chest. I use a flat muscle called the **diaphragm** to breathe. This muscle is below the lungs.

Air in

Ribs move out

Diaphragm moves down

⌃ A balloon gets bigger as it fills with air. My lungs also swell when I breathe in air.

⌄ My ribs move outwards when I breathe in. They move inwards when I breathe out.

Air out

Ribs move in

Diaphragm moves up

⌃ People who have asthma use an inhaler. The inhaler contains medicine to help them breathe more easily.

My lungs transfer some of the oxygen in the air to my blood. I breathe out air that has had the oxygen removed.

35

Heart and blood

My heart is a muscle that pumps blood all around my body. Blood carries vital supplies of oxygen and food, and fights infections.

>> Inside the body is a network of tubes that carry the blood to and from the heart.

⌃ I can feel blood moving through my body at my wrist.

Blood is pumped away from my heart in tubes called **arteries**. Blood flows back to my heart through tubes called **veins**.

Blood collects oxygen from my lungs before it is pumped around my body. When the oxygen is used up, the blood travels back to my heart. It is then pumped to my lungs to pick up more oxygen.

Out

In

Vein

Artery

⌃ My heart is about the same size as my fist. It is here, in the middle of my chest.

Blood filled with oxygen comes from the lungs to the heart.

What is blood?

Blood is a red liquid inside me that keeps me alive. It is made of red and white cells, and smaller cells called platelets, all floating in a fluid called plasma.

Platelets

<< Doctors sometimes take a small amount of blood from a patient. The blood helps them to find out what is wrong with the person.

If your skin is damaged, blood oozes from tiny tubes called **capillaries**. Platelets in the blood thicken and form a scab while your skin is healing.

⋁ **If your skin is bleeding, wash it carefully and cover it with a clean plaster.**

White blood cell

Red blood cell

« **Red blood cells carry oxygen. White blood cells fight diseases and infections.**

Why do I eat?

I get hungry because my body needs food to stay alive. My body uses food so I can grow and to give me energy.

⌄ **Eating** protein **helps me to grow taller. Fish, eggs and beans are all foods that contain protein.**

>> **Playing football uses a lot of energy.**

Foods such as bread and pasta contain **carbohydrates**, which can be turned into energy. Fruits and vegetables contain vitamins, which keep me healthy.

⌃ **A balanced diet has plenty of carbohydrates, protein, calcium and vitamins.**

In my mouth

I chew most food before I swallow it. My teeth crush the food and my tongue mixes it with **saliva**. Then I swallow.

I have 20 baby teeth. When I grow older they will fall out and be replaced by 32 permanent teeth.

>> Brushing my teeth twice a day helps to keep them clean.

Canines are pointed teeth that grip food.

∧ My incisor teeth help me to bite into an apple.

Molars are teeth with flat, bumpy tops that crush food.

Incisors are sharp teeth that slice into food.

43

Into my stomach

When I swallow, food and drink go down a special tube into my stomach. My stomach stretches as I eat.

∨ The walls of my stomach push my food around. They act like a very slow food mixer.

« Food such as yoghurt is easy for my body to digest.

Food mixes with liquids in my stomach to make a thick soup that is easy to digest. A strong **acid** in my stomach helps to dissolve food.

Liver processes digested food

Food tube

Stomach

Intestine

Digesting my food

The thick soup in my stomach passes into my **small intestine**. This is where I digest most of my food and where the nutrients pass into my blood.

« Digestion begins in the mouth. My saliva contains chemicals that start to digest the food.

Stomach

« Food takes up to two days to pass through my digestive system.

Time in the stomach

↓

4 to 5 hours

↓

In the small intestines

↓

About 5 hours

↓

In the large intestines

↓

30-40 hours

↓

Total digestion time

↓

About 2 days

The rest of my food travels on into my **large intestine**. Here it slowly becomes more solid and forms poo.

˄ Poo leaves my body through my anus. Poo contains germs so I always wash my hands after using the toilet.

• Small intestine

• Large intestine

•••••• Anus

47

Why do I drink water?

I drink because my body needs to take in lots of water every day. All drinks contain water and so does food.

>> **More than half my body is water! Every part of me contains some water.**

I need water to replace the water that I lose in **urine** (wee), poo and sweat. Water keeps my body healthy and stops some parts drying out.

>> Fruit and vegetables are mostly water. Squeezing them makes lots of juice to drink.

<< My eyes need tears to keep them wet and clean. When I get upset, I cry lots of tears.

Doing a wee

Wee is one way of getting rid of things my body does not need. My kidneys make urine by taking water and waste substances from my blood.

The urine trickles down tubes to my bladder. My bladder stretches as it fills up. Then I go to the toilet and wee.

<< Babies and toddlers wear nappies because they do not know when their bladder is going to empty.

<< This is how my body produces urine.

Kidneys make urine

Bladder stores urine

Urine leaves my body through a tube

⌃ Urine is usually transparent and yellow.

A new baby

A new baby begins life in its mother's **womb**. This is a special place inside her body. As the baby grows, the mother's womb stretches to form a bump.

>> A newborn baby is almost helpless, but its muscles gradually become stronger and it learns how to move on its own.

When the baby is ready to be born, the mother gives birth. The baby leaves the womb along a passage called the birth canal.

◄ This woman has a baby growing inside her womb.

⌃ This baby is feeding on milk made in its mother's breasts.

Growing older

Children grow from babies into toddlers and then into children who go to school.

∧ A child learns to read, write and count at school.

∧ A baby learns to sit up, crawl and walk.

∧ A toddler begins to use words and grows taller and stronger.

∧ A schoolchild learns about the world and makes friends with other children.

As older children become teenagers, their bodies change. Girls become women and boys become men.

⌃ A teenager's body slowly changes to that of an adult.

⌃ An adult leaves home and may form a family of their own.

⌃ An elderly person begins to slow down and their body becomes weaker.

Healthy way of life

I can help to keep my body working well. Exercise makes my muscles, bones, heart and lungs stronger.

« I make sure I eat five helpings of different fruit and vegetables every day.

I eat lots of different types of food
so that my body gets everything
it needs to be fit and healthy.
I also drink lots of water.

⌃ Running exercises my body. It makes my heart beat faster, which helps it to stay healthy.

Looking after myself

I look after myself to feel good and stay as healthy as possible. Sometimes I get ill, but because I am strong and eat well, I should get better soon.

>> I get a good night's sleep every night.

>> I keep my hair clean by washing it regularly.

58

I keep my body clean by washing and showering. I also make sure I sleep for eight to ten hours a night.

>> I have my teeth checked regularly by the dentist.

Glossary

acid A liquid in the stomach that helps to dissolve food.

arteries The tubes that carry blood from the heart to different parts of the body.

asthma When the airways in the lungs become tight, making it hard for air to pass through them.

brain The part of the body that controls almost everything the body does.

capillaries Very thin tubes that carry blood to every part of your body.

carbohydrates A substance found in many foods, which a body uses to produce energy.

chemicals Substances that occur in nature and are found in our bodies.

diaphragm A flat muscle beneath the lungs that helps us to breathe.

digest To break down food in the body into useful substances.

eardrum Skin that stretches across the ear canal and divides the outer ear from the middle ear.

energy The ability to be active.

iris The coloured ring around the pupil of the eye.

joint A part of the body where two or more bones meet.

large intestine The tube that undigested food passes along before it leaves the body as poo.

lens A part of the eye that bends light to form a picture.

lungs The body part where oxygen from the air passes into the blood.

muscles The parts of the body that move, or move other body parts.

nerves Thin threads that carry messages to and from the brain.

oxygen One of the gases found in air, which we need to stay alive.

protein A substance found in many foods, which helps a body to grow.

pupil The dark hole in the eye through which light passes.

saliva The liquid made in the mouth. It is also called spit.

senses Messages sent from the body to the brain that tell you what is going on around you. There are five main senses: seeing, hearing, touch, taste and smell.

small intestine The long, thin tube in which most of our food is digested.

sound wave A vibration in the air that we sense with our ears.

sweat A liquid made in the skin to help you to cool down.

taste buds Places on the tongue that form the sense of taste.

urine A yellow liquid that leaves the body when you wee.

veins The tubes that carry blood back to the heart from different parts of the body.

waterproof Not allowing water to pass through.

womb The part of a woman's body where a baby forms and grows until it is born.

Index

Picture credits

(t=top, b=bottom, l=left, r=right, c=centre, fc=front cover, bc=back cover)

Dreamstime.com
4 bl Anke Van Wyk, 5 Eveleen007, 10 cr Dmitry Kalinovsky, 16–17 Tinnakorn Srivichai, 18 bl Dmitry Naumov, 18–19 Jimmyi23, 19 tr Varina And Jay Patel, 22 bl Michael Gray, 24 bc Sebastian Kaulitzki, 24–25 Science Pics, 27 tr Giovanni Caito, 28 cl Sebastian Kaulitzki, 28–29 Ia64, 29 tr Sam74100, 29 br FabioConcetta, 30 bl Serrnovik, 31 br Tomasz Markowski, 32 cr Mashiki, 33 tr Creostudio, 34 bl Dimitri Surkov, 37 tr Syda Productions, 39 bl Jean Paul Chassenet, 39 br Greenland, 40–41 Jorg Hackemann, 42 cl Pavla Zakova, 42 br Rmarmion, 44 bl Sinisha Karich, 44 br Kiosea39, 46 bl Tanyaru, 46–47 Elenabsl, 47 br Pipa100, 48–49 Handmademedia, 49 tl Ekaterina Dushenina, 51 cr Jean Paul Chassenet, 52 b Oksun70, 52–53 Diego Vito Cervo, 53 br Feije Riemersma, 57 cb Aas2009

iStock.com
1 c Alina Solovyova-Vincent, 2 bl Kobyakov, 4 br Sasiistock, 6 bl Wavebreakmedia, 6 br Maartje van Caspel, 7 PhotoEuphoria, 8–9 Milan Zeremski, 10 bl medlar, 12 bl Renphoto, 13 br Necip Yanmaz, 14 bl ajfletch, 15 tr Kobyakov, 16 bl HeikeKampe, 17 cr jackscoldsweat, 20 bl ToddKuhns, 20–21 Fertnig, 21 tr Aslan Alphan, 22–23 Michael Krinke, 23 cr BradCalkins, 25 br leonello, 26 bl Ampack, 26 r Andrew Rich, 32 bl Paul Gregg, 35 tr CT757fan, 25 bl caimacanul, 38–39 Eraxion , 40 bl Tagstock1, 41 br Christopher Futcher, 49 b GMVozd, 50 bl jonas unruh, 56 bl RTimages, 56–57 kirin_photo, 58 cb onebluelight, 58–59 aabejon, 59 br Steex, 63 br jonas unruh

Shutterstock
8 b Sebastian Kaulitzki